I0490755

Gift Card Pro

Buy, Sell, Save, and Trade Discounted Gift Cards

Author: Michael Cruz

v. 1.0014G

International Standard Book Number
ISBN: 979-83873444-04

Published by:
RMC Digital Holdings, LLC
3515 Atlantic Avenue #1045
Long Beach, California 90807 USA
support@importantadvice.com

Published in the United States of America

Disclaimer

The information and data herein represent the publisher's view of the publication date. Because of the rate with which conditions change, the publisher reserves the right to alter and update an opinion based on the new/updated conditions. This report is for informational purposes only.

While every attempt has been made to verify the information provided in this report, neither the publisher nor affiliates/partners assume any responsibility for errors, inaccuracies, or omissions. Any slights of people or organizations are unintentional. If advice concerning legal or related matters is needed, the services of a fully qualified professional should be sought.

This publication is not intended for use as a source of legal, accounting, or financial/ investment advice. You should be aware of any laws which govern business transactions or other business practices in your area.

Any trademarks, copyrights, designs, and imaging used in this publication are the property of their respective owners. We are grateful for their contribution.

An Important Message to My Readers

First and foremost, thank you for purchasing *Gift Card Pro*.

It seemed daunting when I decided to take on the challenge of writing this book. First was the extensive research for credible gift card resellers and then locating quality resources who can help make your gift card quest a success.

I care about providing a quality product that makes you more financially secure. If, for any reason, you find anything within the publication worthy of commenting on, please bring this to my attention. I have placed hyperlinks throughout this publication to help you locate additional information. Websites sometimes change URLs, so if you notice a link that's not operational, please let us know: support@importantadvice.com.

Be sure to visit our website: ImportantAdvice.com/updates, to receive updates on gift cards and other tools and resources that may help you. It may start with limited content but be assured that I want to provide value to my audience. Cheers!

Michael Cruz

Access to Links

With over 100 links in the book, you have access to vetted resources to help make your gift card experiences a success.

Please use a mobile device to scan the QR code <u>on the last page</u> of this publication. You will receive a PDF containing all the links embedded in the eBook version.

Need help? Please send us an email we'll be happy to assist you.

<u>support@importantadvice.com</u>
Gift Card Pro

Table of Contents

Gift Card Pro

Overview

When someone thinks of Neiman Marcus, it usually evokes images of elegant fashion, luxurious furnishings, and other incomparable merchandise, but not gift cards. Yet, amazingly, Neiman Marcus was the first American retailer to launch pre-paid debit cards, known as gift cards, in 1994.

A year later, Blockbuster Video launched gift cards on a nationwide scale. They were physical cards that customers could purchase and redeem for rental items or snacks in the store. It was also an excellent replacement for those pesky, easy-to-counterfeit paper gift certificates.

Today, gift card sales have become a $534 billion annual industry. They are a wildly popular alternative to traditional gifts, particularly for those who are challenging to shop for. Gift cards also offer convenience for the giver since they do not have to spend time choosing a specific gift.

In a recent survey, over 57% of participants said they would prefer a gift card over a physical item.

The *National Retail Federation* states that 81% of all Americans have given or received a gift card at least once. Gift cards can also be used as a way for businesses to promote their products or services. Luckily for merchants, not all gift cards are redeemed—for various reasons.

CNBC reported that a whopping 47% of gift card owners eventually lose out on gift money. That represents a portion of merchants' profits. In 2019, Starbucks announced in its annual report a $140 million gain from unused gift cards; department store Nordstrom had $17 million; and The Cheesecake Factory received $8 million, referred to as "breakage."

According to Wikipedia, National Use Your Gift Card Day is a shopping holiday in the US that takes place yearly on the third Saturday of January. It is an unofficial observance with an inaugural date of January 18, 2020. The day is utilized to encourage people to use their gift cards. The idea gained traction in retail, with major chains supporting the holiday.

Physical and Digital Gift Cards
There are key differences between physical and digital gift cards.

Physical gift cards are usually purchased in a store. Depending on the card's terms, they can be used in-store or online at participating retailers. Physical gift cards are typically made of plastic and can have a company logo, design, or message.

Digital gift cards, or e-gift cards, are often delivered with a numerical or QR code that can be used at the checkout to redeem the card's value.

One significant difference between physical and digital gift cards is the delivery method. Physical gift cards must be mailed or hand-delivered, while digital gift cards can be delivered instantly via email or text. This makes digital gift cards a convenient option for last-minute gift giving or for recipients who live far away.

Customized Gift Cards

Anyone can buy a gift card off the rack, but customized gift cards allow you to send a personalized message.

It's a simple process: Upload an original photo and text, so each gift card is personally designed for the recipient. They can be sent for any occasion, such as a birthday, Valentine's Day, or graduation.

Customized gift cards are becoming increasingly popular with the younger generations. Here are a few vendors who offer customized gift cards:

GiftCards.com
GiftCard Granny
Amazon
Vanilla Gift Card

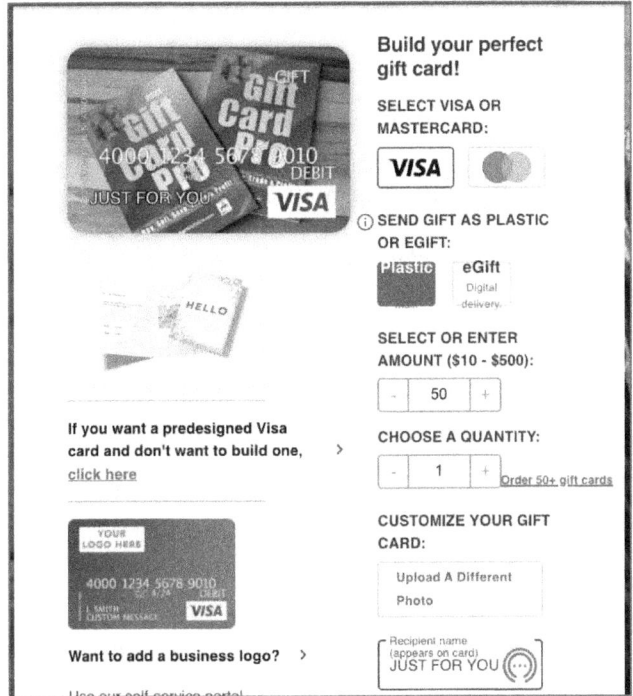

Best Selling Gift Cards

Amazon
Walmart
Home Depot
Best Buy
Lowes
Foot Locker
Nike
Starbucks
Nordstrom
Bed, Bath & Beyond
Sam's Club
Dick's Sporting Goods
Sephora
Apple
Kohl's
eBay

An Act of Congress

Because gift cards grew in popularity quickly, it was only a matter of time before states, and Congress got into the act. As a result, gift cards are regulated at the federal and state level. On the national front, the Credit CARD Act of 2009 established several protections for consumers who use gift cards which include:

No expiration dates: Gift cards cannot expire within five years of being issued or from when funds are last added to the card.

No *fees:* Gift cards can only have activation, maintenance, or dormancy fees if the card has not been used for at least one year. A price must be disclosed to the consumer if it is charged.

Balance disclosure: If a gift card balance is requested, the issuer must disclose the credit to the consumer free of charge.

Replacement: If a gift card is lost, stolen, or damaged, the issuer must replace the card or the remaining balance on the card at no cost to the consumer. A paper receipt is usually required for this type of transaction.

In addition to these federal protections, several states have laws regulating gift cards. These laws may include additional protections, such as prohibiting expiration dates or fees on gift cards or requiring that the remaining balance on a gift card be refunded to the consumer if the balance falls below a certain amount.

This is discussed further in Gift Card Pro #29—Cash Redemption.

Most popular types of Gift Cards

- *Store Gift Cards* allow you to shop at a specific retail store or chain of stores. These cards are often reloadable, meaning you can use them multiple times. They are ideal for those who want the flexibility to shop at multiple locations.

- *Restaurant Gift Cards* can be used at specific restaurants or chains of restaurants. These cards can be easily reloaded whenever desired and are perfect for foodies who love trying new things.

- *Cinema Gift Cards* can purchase movie tickets or rentals at a specific theatre or chain of theaters. They are ideal for cinema enthusiasts.

- *E-Gift Cards,* or *digital* or *virtual cards,* can be used to shop at certain online retailers. They are convenient for those who prefer to shop from the comfort of their own home.

- *Travel Gift Cards* can be used to book travel accommodation or airfare. Are you looking for a getaway? Travel gift cards allow you to explore new places and are ideal for frequent commuters or travelers.

- *Gas Gift Cards* can be used to purchase gas at specific stations or chains of stations.

- *General Purpose Gift Cards* can be used <u>anywhere</u> that accepts major credit cards. They are most commonly branded as Visa, MasterCard, and American Express. These cards are only sometimes reloadable and offer the greatest flexibility for use anywhere.

Just the Gift Card Facts and Stats

Gift cards represent a huge industry that continues to grow annually. In a quest to dig up some interesting facts and figures, I found that the higher your income, the more likely you'll have purchased or received a digital gift card.

Your home location can also make a big difference to whether you have purchased or obtained a digital gift card. Midwesterners are less likely to have purchased a digital gift card than their Eastern and Western counterparts.

E-gifting is the fastest-growing segment of gift cards.

Here are some other interesting statistics...

81% of American consumers have given or received a gift card

73% said they would purchase a gift card during the 2022 holiday season

62% of gift card purchasers use digital gift cards as last-minute gifts

53% said they would be interested in storing gift cards on their phones

26% annual growth in gift cards

8% will convert their gift cards into cash

$3 billion every year wasted with unused gift cards

2 is the average number of gift cards consumers purchased in 2022

$1 trillion market is expected by 2030.

Unwanted Gift Cards

There will always be a certain number of people who receive gift cards who would rather have the cash than the gift card itself. According to Card Cash, that number represents about 8% of all gift cards purchased. Considering that over $534 billion in gift cards were bought last year, <u>billions in unwanted gift cards end up on the secondary market each year.</u>

Unwanted gift cards can save on goods and services you probably already use. As you'll discover, there are quality outlets for purchasing gift cards online and several undesirable outlets. Rather than you wasting time, we have vetted all the online resources available in this publication.

Other Key Points

Savings from discounted gift cards can add up fast. When you get down to it, there is only one way to "save" money: <u>not spending it</u>. Making multiple efforts to save small amounts of money can lead to a substantial lump sum in your savings account.

Take advantage of small saving opportunities when they arise. Anytime you can extend and maximize your savings, it may take a minor effort, but it is rewarding.

Discounted cards help fight inflation. According to the Federal Reserve, the year 2022 had a 6.5% increase in the inflation rate. While gift cards cannot cover your utilities or home mortgage, you can use them in many areas. The median savings of discounted gift cards average 12.7% off the total face value. That's almost $13 saved for every $100 spent.

Gift *card sellers can expect to receive around 70–80% value of the card.* In other words, the seller will receive about 70 to 80 cents on the dollar. The exact amount depends on the discount outlet's inventory and the retailer's popularity.

How Gift Card Pro is set-up

This book is broken into six categories:

(1) Card Professional

Twelve awesome hacks on getting the most from gift cards. Discover where to save up to 35% on selected gift cards, manage all your gift cards in a mobile app, and even find ways to convert your gift card to cash.

(2) Discount Trader

This is for you if you're seeking the best-discounted gift card marketplaces online. In most cases, you can buy discounted cards and sell unwanted gift cards on most platforms.

(3) Extended Value

This is where savings start to add up! It's always great when you can save money on discounted gift cards, but getting added value, such as using a retailer's loyalty program or coupons, is even better.

(4) Amazon

One of the most popular gift cards on the planet, Amazon, deserves to be in its own category. Discover a few innovative ways to use your Amazon gift card.

(5) Locals Only

This includes local-based marketplaces such as Facebook. Trade-in programs with Target, Best Buy, and other resources simplify buying, selling, or trading your gift cards in your local area.

(6) Miscellaneous

Some necessary and random gift card tips and tricks you can employ

Category: Card Professional

Card Professional has the top 12 most valuable resources, including the two discount resellers of gift cards and powerful hacks to help you save when shopping.

GIFT CARD PRO #01
Real Deal: CardCash.com
Digital GCs: Yes
Mobile App: Yes
Loyalty: Yes
Tracking: Yes

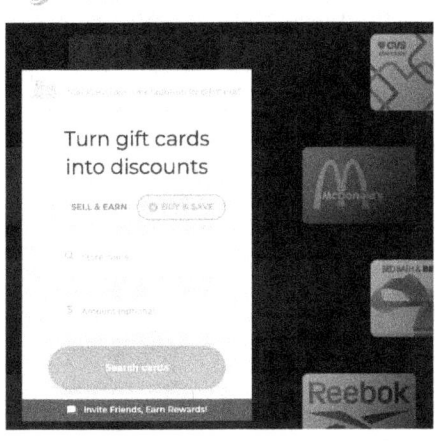

With an inventory of over 520 branded gift cards, CardCash.com is one of the leading websites for buying, selling, and exchanging gift cards.

Since 2009, CardCash has bought gift cards from individuals and businesses at a discounted price and then resold them at a slightly higher price, but still lower than the face value of the card. CardCash also offers a price-matching guarantee and a rewards program for frequent shoppers. This is where customers can earn points on purchases redeemed for discounts. There's even free shipping for physical gift cards.

Their website states, "CardCash has the world's largest inventory of discounted gift cards and, since its inception, has saved customers more than $50 million from their favorite retail brands." In addition, the discount reseller says 85% of gift cards sold on the CardCash website are digital e-gift cards.

Oddly enough, CardCash will allow you to exchange your gift card for an Amazon gift card, but they do not sell Amazon-branded gift cards on their platform.

Here's a broad sample of discounted gift cards available on CardCash:

Toppers Spa/Salon	35%	Day spa treatments
Red Box	30%	Entertainment
Jos A. Bank	28%	Quality men's wear
Oakley Eyewear	28%	Personal accessories
Harley-Davidson	21%	Hobby accessories
Helzberg Diamonds	22%	Watches/jewelry
Zales Jewelers	15%	Watches/Jewelry
1-800-Flowers	14%	Florist
Movie-Tickets	21%	Movies
AMC Theaters	15%	Movies
Macaroni Grill	26%	Night on the town
Black Angus	20%	Night on the town
Applebees	17%	Family Restaurant
Chili's	16%	Bar and grill
NASCAR	29%	Hobby savings
NFL Shop	23%	Hobby savings
Calloway Golf	18%	Hobby savings
Bass Pro Shops	11%	Hobby savings
Krispy Donuts	22%	Office-group gathering
Pet Supplies	15%	Part of the family
CVS	4%	Pharmacy & food Items
Rite Aid	18%	Lower Prescriptions
Walgreens	11%	Pharmacy
Home Depot	4%	Home improvement
Lowes	5%	Home improvement
Lumber Liquidators	15%	Small house projects
Celebrity Cruises	14%	Vacation-getaways
Hotels.com	6%	Vacation-getaways

Other Popular Retailers:

Starbucks	4% + loyalty and app
Target	2% + loyalty, app and in-store promos
McDonald's	3% + loyalty via app
Home Depot	4% + loyalty and app

These discounted numbers were compiled at CardCash.com on December 27, 2022. The discounted percentages and availability are subject to change without notice. Limited-time promotions may not be valid on the apps. Check promotional emails to learn their terms and conditions.

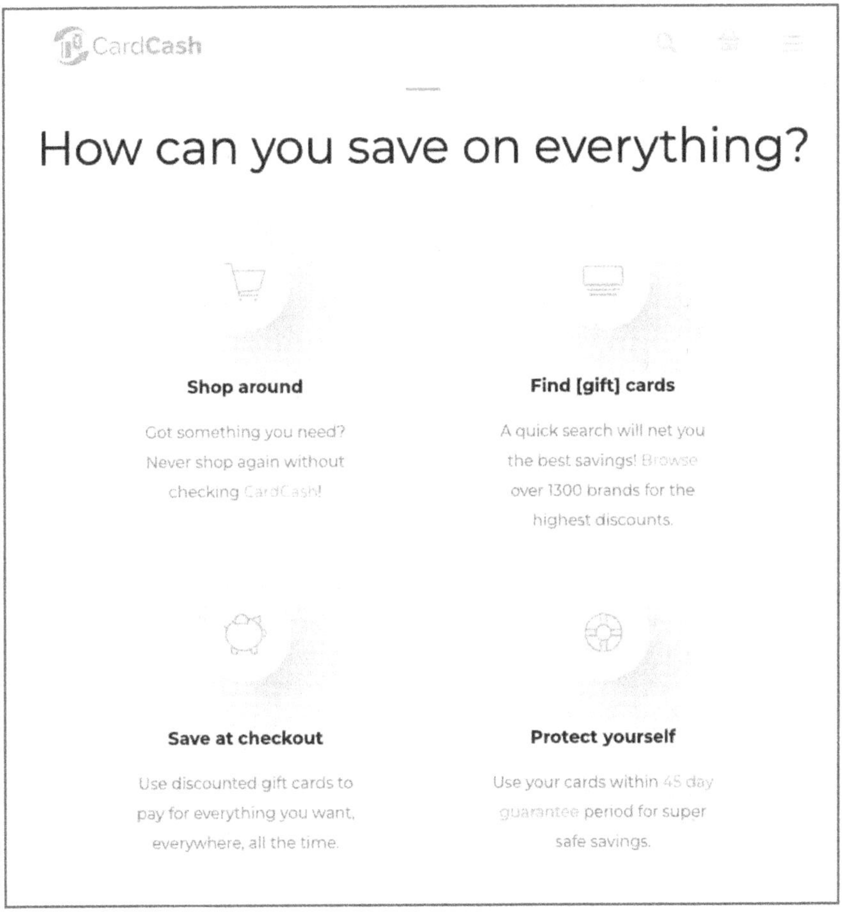

CardCash

How can you save on everything?

Shop around

Got something you need?
Never shop again without
checking CardCash!

Find [gift] cards

A quick search will net you
the best savings! Browse
over 1300 brands for the
highest discounts.

Save at checkout

Use discounted gift cards to
pay for everything you want,
everywhere, all the time.

Protect yourself

Use your cards within 45 day
guarantee period for super
safe savings.

Download the CashCash mobile app

GIFT CARD PRO #02
Real Deal: Raise.com
Digital GCs: Yes
Mobile App: Yes
Loyalty: Yes
Tracking: Yes

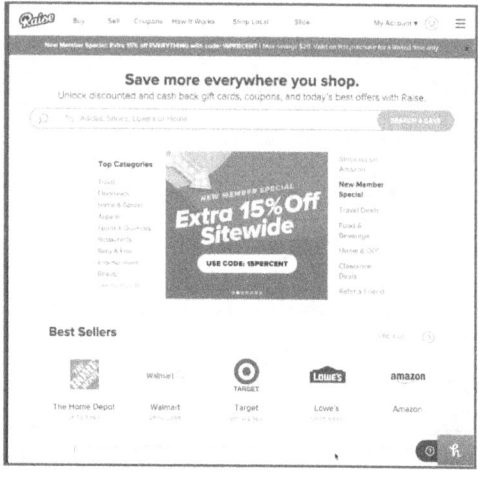

Similar to CardCash, Raise.com is a reputable clearinghouse for discounted gift cards.

They continually run a $5 promotion when a new user signs up. During the post-holiday season, this amount may increase for a specific time.

With Raise, you can save up to 30% on their marketplace-discounted gift cards from many brands. All gift cards are electronic and delivered instantly. Depending on the brand, electronic cards may be redeemed online or in-store. Double-check during the checkout process to review specific delivery and redemption instructions.

Other benefits of Raise include:

Earn cash back. Get Raise Cash instantly for over 150 retail partners when someone buys face-value cards. Enter the amount you'd like to pay, and they will apply earnings to future orders.

Pay in-store or online. Most cards are delivered electronically within minutes. Log into your Raise account online or download the Raise app to access and redeem your cards on the go!

Provides a one-year money-back guarantee, which is a great deal. That's a whole 365 days; your gift card is guaranteed.

Pay and save on the go with Raise. Download the Raise app to shop, store, and redeem your cards anytime. The app is available on desktops and mobile devices.

Stack your savings with discounted and cash back gift cards and coupons.

DISCOUNT

Buy discounted gift cards for yourself and save up to 30% at thousands of your favorite stores.

SAVE NOW

CASH BACK

Buy full-priced gift cards and get up to 15% back in Raise Cash to spend on future purchases.

EARN NOW

COUPONS

Unlock even more savings with promo codes, free shipping, and today's top deals for your favorite brands.

BROWSE NOW

Download the raise app:

GIFT CARD PRO #03
Real Deal: 8 Ways to Convert GCs Into Cash

After the holidays and throughout the year, many are looking to cash out their gift card for various reasons.

CNBC says recipients can quickly turn gift cards into cash (or more desirable gift cards) through reputable sites like Raise and CardCash. The site you choose will depend on the ease of sale and your gift card type. You won't get total value for it, but that's better than letting a gift card go unused.

Here are six additional ways to convert your gift card into cash:

GiftCardBin. Over 600 partner locations. Take your gift cards with a valid ID to their location and get cash for your gift cards.

GiftCard Granny. Multiple options are available: (1) list card on their marketplace to choose the best offer, (2) list card for a set price, or (3) exchange the existing card for one you actually want.

Gift Card Spread. The seller decides the price for the gift card by completing an online form. The website will confirm the amount or possibly provide a counteroffer. A valid ID is required for all transactions.

EJgiftCards. The site claims to offer the highest payouts for your gift cards and store credit based on the current market rates. There is no limit on the number of gift cards you can cash out and no limit on the gift card balance.

QuickCashMI. The website states they will buy gift cards for up to 90%. Unfortunately, their service does not provide electronic payments to first-time customers.

BuyBackWorld. This platform provides an instant offer for unwanted gift cards. If you accept, a prepaid shipping label is used to mail your gift cards to their office. It takes about three days for a payout.

TIP: Gift card kiosks tend to lower the exchange values after the holiday season.

GIFT CARD PRO #04
Real Deal: Transfer Gift Card Funds to App

If you have an all-purpose gift card such as a Visa/MasterCard/Amex, you can transfer it to your bank or into apps such as PayPal, Venmo, and other digital wallets.

Cash App

1. Open the Cash App, click on the '+,' then select 'Add Bank'.

2. Enter the gift card information.

3. Tap on the gift card button 'Balance' and select 'Cash Out'. Enter the amount you wish to transfer from your gift card to your bank account.

PayPal

1. Log in and select 'Wallet' at the top of the page.

2. Select 'Link a card or bank account'.

3. Enter the gift card number, date, and CID.

5. Click 'Link Card'.

6. Once the card is in PayPal's system, click 'Withdraw' and select 'Transfer to Bank Account.'

Venmo

1. Open the app and select 'Payment.'

2. Click the 'Withdraw' button, then select 'Gift Card' to withdraw.

3. Enter the amount to withdraw into your bank account.

MoneyGram

1. Log in and enter the amount you want to transfer from a gift card.

2. Select 'Gift Card' as payment.

3. Enter your bank account information.

4. Click 'Send' to transfer money to a bank account.

GIFT CARD PRO #05
Real Deal: GiftCardWiki.com

GiftCardWiki is a platform that provides information on gift cards, including their availability, value, and terms and conditions. It also offers a marketplace where users can buy, sell, and exchange gift cards. One of the coolest advantages of this platform is seeing how other resellers rate all in one place.

With GiftCardWiki, you can benefit in several ways:

1. *First, get the best value for your gift card:* GiftCardWiki provides real-time updates on various gift card platforms. This lets you make informed decisions when selling or exchanging your gift cards, ensuring you get the best value.

2. *Access various gift cards:* GiftCardWiki offers many gift cards from popular retailers and brands. So whether you're looking for a gift for someone special or want to treat yourself, you're sure to find a gift card that meets your needs on GiftCardWiki.

3. *Buy and sell gift cards securely:* GiftCardWiki provides a secure platform for buying, selling, and exchanging gift cards. When using the platform, you can be confident that your transactions are safe and secure.

4. *Find gift cards at a discount*: GiftCardWiki often has gift cards available at a deal, which can help you save money on your purchases. You can buy gift cards for a fraction of their face value and use them to purchase goods and services at their total value.

5. *Stay informed on gift card trends:* GiftCardWiki provides articles and resources on gift cards, including the latest trends and news. This lets you stay updated on the world of gift cards and make informed decisions when buying, selling, or exchanging them.

To sum up, GiftCardWiki is a valuable resource for anyone interested in gift cards. Using the platform, you can save money, access various gift cards, and make informed decisions about your gift card transactions.

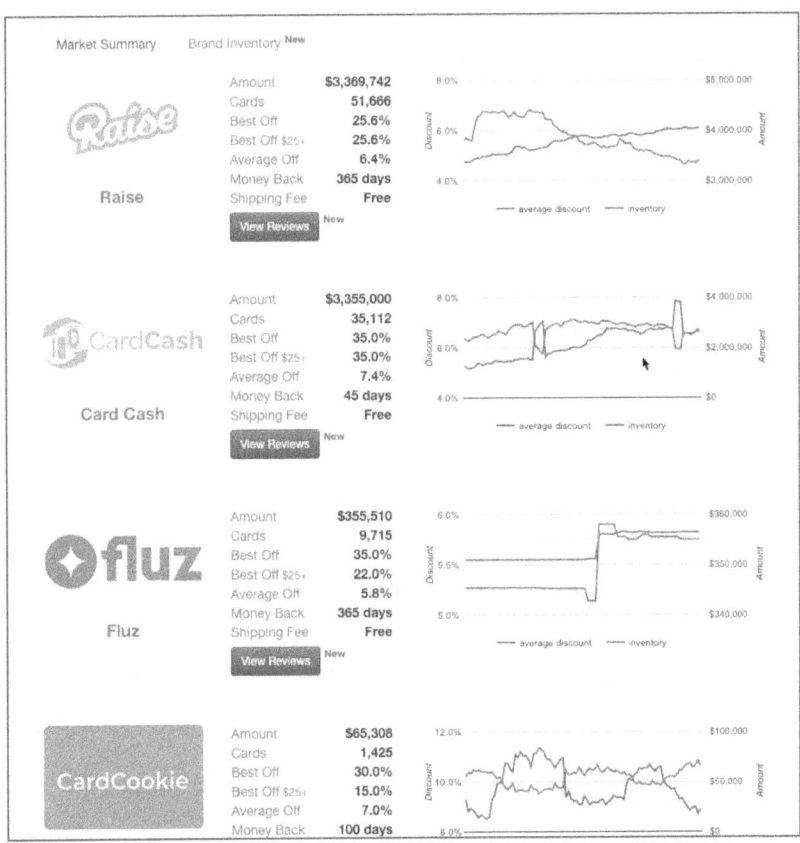

GIFT CARD PRO #06
Real Deal: Gift Card Bulk Buys

If you are about to incur a major expense such as a home improvement project, wedding, or significant catering event, buying gift cards in bulk is the real deal. Besides, you will spend the money regardless, so why not save?

Purchase gift cards in bulk can offer several advantages, including:

1. *Cost savings*: By purchasing gift cards in bulk, you can often receive a discount on the face value of the cards, resulting in cost savings. The average savings can vary depending on the retailer and the volume of gift cards purchased, ranging from 5% to 25%.

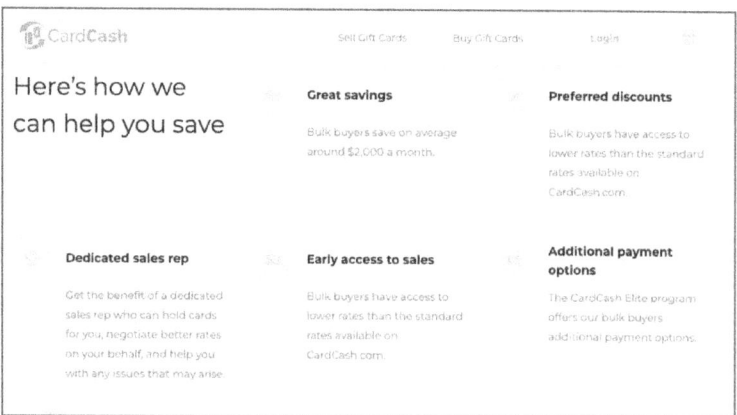

2. *Convenient gifting option*: Buying gift cards in bulk can be suitable for those looking to give gifts to a large group of people. With gift cards, recipients can choose their gifts, and you can purchase them all at once, saving time and effort.

3. *Easy to store*: Gift cards are small and easy to store, making it easy to keep a large quantity of them on hand for future use.

To buy gift cards in bulk, the requirements may vary depending on the retailer, but generally, you need to meet the following:

1.　Have a business account: Many retailers require businesses to open a special account to purchase bulk gift cards. (Check with each platform).

2.　Meet minimum purchase requirements: Some retailers may have a minimum requirement, so checking this before bulk purchasing is essential.

3.　Provide payment information: You must provide payment information to purchase gift cards in bulk.

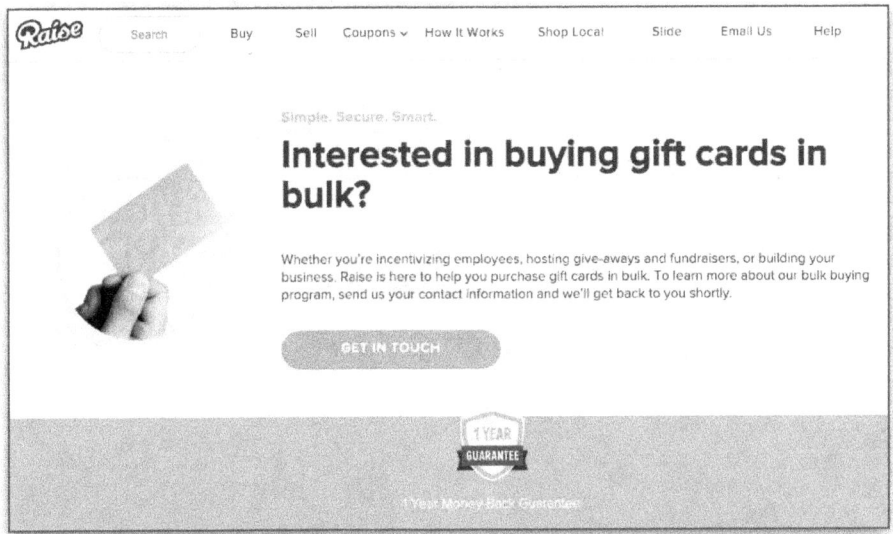

You can buy gift cards in bulk from several sources, including:

1.　Retailers: Many retailers, such as Amazon, Target, and Walmart, offer bulk gift card purchases for businesses.

2.　Gift card resellers: Companies specializing in selling gift cards, such as CardCash and Raise, offer bulk gift card purchases at a discount.

3.　Corporate incentives companies: Companies specializing in corporate incentives and rewards often offer bulk gift card purchases as part of their services.

It is important to thoroughly research the retailer or gift card reseller before making a bulk purchase to ensure you receive a quality product at a fair price.

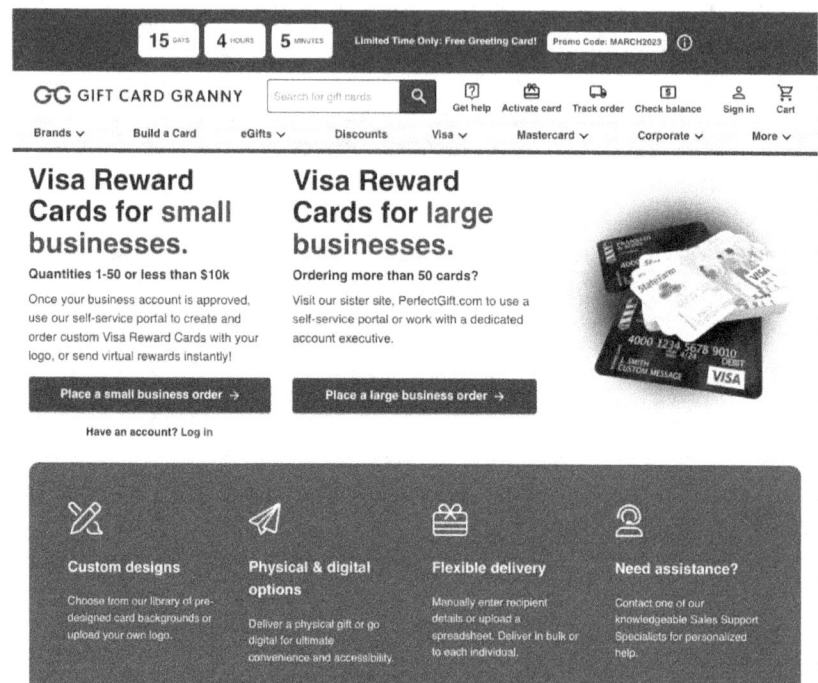

GIFT CARD PRO #07
Real Deal: The Gyft App

With the Gyft mobile app, you can **manage, store, and check the balance of your plastic gift cards**. You can conveniently redeem your gift cards in stores straight from your mobile phone.

Got a gift card that you don't want? With Gyft, you can always re-gift gift cards you have received but will not use.

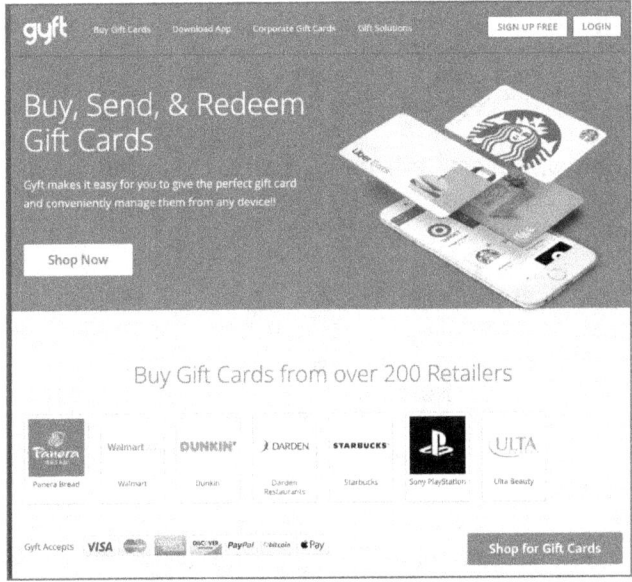

Download the Gyft app:

TIP: Have too many apps on your phone? No problem; take a photo of your physical gift cards and store them on your phone so you can retrieve the number when needed.

GIFT CARD PRO #08
Real Deal: Multiple Partners

This is one of my favorite hacks because you can save money by purchasing gift cards accepted at multiple retailer brands. For example, a Gap gift card is also accepted at Old Navy and Banana Republic. So, if a Gap card is discounted at 10% off, look for Old Navy or Banana Republic gift cards with a higher discount offered instead.

As shown below, several gift cards can be used at multiple brands, allowing users to shop at various stores or businesses with a single card. Here are a few stores that accept each other's gift cards:

- **Kroger brand stores**: Kroger, Barclay Jewelers, Baker's, City Market, Copps, Dillons, Food 4 Less, Foods Co., Fred Meyer, Fred Meyer Jewelers, Fresh Eats, Fry's Food and Drug, Gerbes, Jay C, King Soopers, Littman Jewelers, Mariano's, Metro Market, Owen's, Pay Less Supermarkets, Pick 'n Save, QFC, Ralphs, Smith's Food and Drug and Turkey Hill Experience
- **Gap**: Gap Kids, Old Navy, Ahela, and Banana Republic
- **Outback Steakhouse**: Carrabba's Italian Grill, Bonefish Grill
- **Williams-Sonoma**: Mark and Graham, Pottery Barn Kids, Pottery Barn, PBteen, and West Elm
- **Walmart:** and Sam's Club (including branded gas stations)
- **J.Crew**: J.Crew Factory, J.Crew Mercantile
- **Abercrombie & Fitch**: Abercrombie Kids
- **Darden Restaurants:** Olive Garden, Bahama Breeze, Long Horn Steakhouse, Red Lobster, Season 52, The Capital Grille, and Yard House.

TIP: When shopping on the Gift Card Granny website, look to the bottom left side of your screen — it will inform you if the cards are accepted at other stores.

GIFT CARD PRO #09
Real Deal: <u>Groupon</u>

Mobile App: Yes
Loyalty: Yes

Groupon will not buy unwanted gift cards, but sometimes you'll see better-discounted deals on Groupon than on gift card sites. After registering as a user, look for discounts that may interest you. Be sure to sign up for their alerts for a specific business you wish to save on.

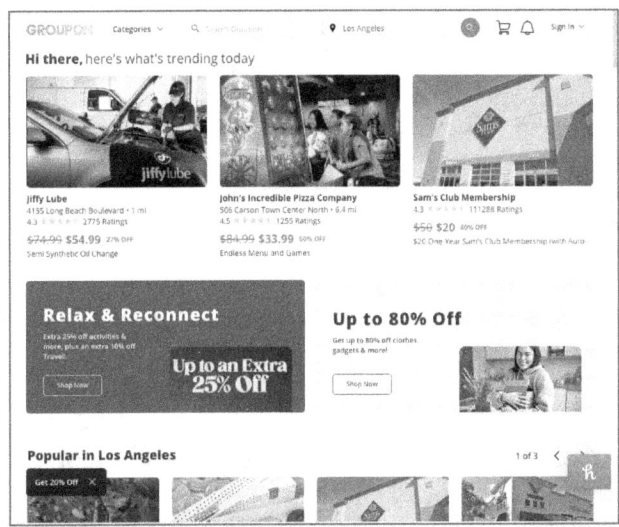

No matter how you look at it, Groupon is a website and app that allows users to find and redeem deals and discounts from various retailers, restaurants, and other locally-owned businesses. So why not sign up today?

Download the app:

TIP: If you plan to travel, check out Groupon deals for your destination.

GIFT CARD PRO #10
Real Deal: Savings on the Go
Digital Cards: Yes
Mobile App: Yes
Loyalty: Yes
Tracking: Yes

According to Pew Research Center, 85% of Americans possess a smartphone, yet, most don't take advantage of purchasing discounted e-gift cards when out shopping.

For example, imagine entering CVS Pharmacy while using your Raise app to buy a digital gift card with 15% off. After a few clicks, the gift card is now on your phone. Then, show the clerk the QR code (or gift card number), and congratulations, you just bought the items you wanted and saved 15 percent off using your smartphone.

Use mobile apps to locate an online reseller with a discount and digital gift cards on the go. Here are a few benefits of using mobile gift card apps such as CardCash, Raise, and Gyft:

1. **Save money:** These apps allow you to buy gift cards at a discounted price, which can save you money on purchases.

2. **Convenient**: With mobile gift card apps, you can buy and redeem gift cards anytime, anywhere.

3. **Easy to use:** Mobile gift card apps are user-friendly and easy to use. You can quickly search for the retailer or brand you're interested in and purchase a gift card with just a few taps on your phone.

4. **Secure:** Mobile gift card apps use secure payment methods to ensure your personal and financial information.

5. **Wide variety of options:** Mobile gift card apps offer various gift card options from multiple retailers and brands. This means you can find the perfect gift card for any occasion.

Start saving money on the go today!

GIFT CARD PRO #11
Real Deal: Card Tracker

Google Alerts is a free service that allows users to receive notifications when new content is published online that matches specific keywords or phrases. Specifically, this will enable you to monitor websites selling specific gift card brands.

With Google Alerts, you'll save time instead of constantly checking sites for a particular gift card.

To sign up for Google Alerts, follow these steps:

1. First, go to the Google Alerts website.
2. Next, sign in to your Google account. If you don't have one, you'll need to create one.
3. Next, enter the keyword or phrase you want to track in the "Create an alert about" field.
4. Next, choose the type of results you wish to receive.
5. Next, decide how often you want to receive alerts (e.g., as-it-happens, once a day, once a week).
6. Finally, select how to receive alerts (e.g., email, RSS feed).
7. Click the "Create Alert" button.

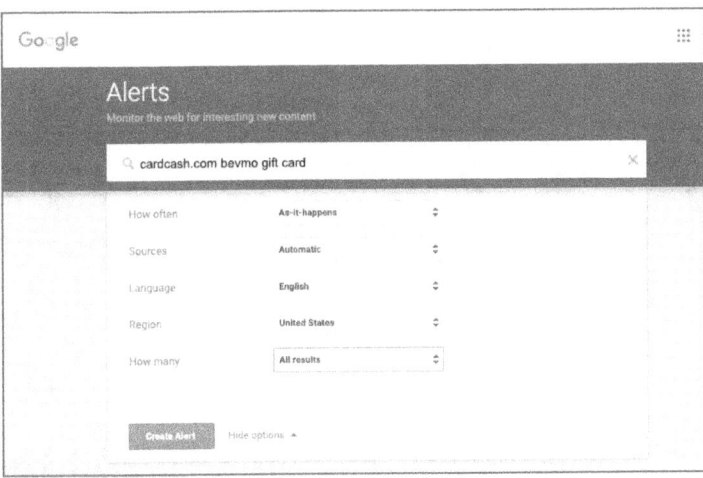

That's it! You'll receive alerts whenever new online content matches your keyword or phrase. You can set up as many alerts as you like and manage or delete them at any time from your Google Alerts dashboard.

GIFT CARD PRO #12
Real Deal: GC Side Hustles

There are two separate ways you can profit from gift cards. The first is a local reseller buying, selling, and trading gift cards, and the second utilizes the Paxful platform. Here's a closer look at each one.

Local Reseller.

Due to the sheer volume of people possessing gift cards, it provides you with a deep pool of prospects. Once you decide your margin (profit) for card transactions, the key is to get the word out. Craig's List and Facebook Marketplace are sure bets to meet potential customers. Business cards are also an essential marketing tool because you can pass them out anywhere, such as a laundromat, grocery store, pharmacy, local tavern, and even after church.

Before you start reselling gift cards, it's essential to do your research and understand the market. Look for high-demand gift cards being sold at a discounted price. It's also a good idea to set a fair price for your gift cards based on the current market value. To maintain credibility, have customers use Facebook Marketplace or Yelp for reviews. The more reviews you receive, the more credible you become with your local prospects.

Paxful is the leading peer-to-peer marketplace that lets you directly trade gift cards for cash or cryptocurrency. The community is 10 million strong and growing every day. Significant discounts can be found, and you can use over 500 methods of buying discounted cards. This scope is much larger than explained here; luckily, Paxful has a course describing how to save money on gift cards.

Category: Discount Trader

GIFT CARD PRO #13
Real Deal: Warehouse Clubs

If you're a member of warehouse sites such as Costco and Sam's Club, you probably know that these two mega-retailers offer discounted gift cards throughout the year. While they are more popular and promoted during the holiday season, you can save up to 35% on selected gift cards all year round.

The only drawback is that you need to be a member, but if you buy plenty of cards for restaurants and selected retailers, the savings can quickly outweigh the membership cost.

TIP: CardCash and Groupon offer steep Sam's Club membership discounts.

Download the Costco app.

Download the Sam's Club app.

GIFT CARD PRO #14

Real Deal: iBotta

Digital Cards: Yes
Mobile App: Yes
Loyalty: Yes
Tracking: Yes

iBotta is a cash-back and rewards website allowing shoppers to earn money back on purchases from participating retailers. The website offers a variety of ways to earn cash back, including shopping online through the iBotta website, scanning receipts from in-store purchases, and completing tasks or surveys.

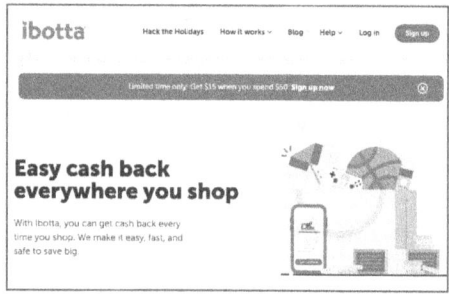

Once you sign up for an iBotta account, you can browse the available offers and select the ones you want to redeem. Then, when you make a qualifying purchase, you can submit your receipt or proof of purchase to iBotta to receive cash back.

In addition to cash-back offers, iBotta offers other rewards, such as coupons and discounts. These can be used to save money on future purchases or to get free or discounted items.

Another benefit of iBotta is that it works with retailers, including major chains and smaller local businesses. This means you can earn cash back on purchases from various places, not just stores or name brands.

iBotta also has a referral program that allows users to invite friends and family to join the platform. When someone you refer signs up and makes a qualifying purchase, you can earn additional cash back or other rewards.

Overall, iBotta is a convenient way for shoppers to earn cash back and save money on purchases from participating retailers. Using the website and app, you can easily track your earnings and redeem your rewards, making it simple and hassle-free to save money on your everyday shopping.

GIFT CARD PRO #15

Real Deal: GiftCards.com

Digital Cards: Yes
Mobile App: No
Loyalty: Yes
Tracking: Yes

Founded in 1999, Giftcards.com offers one of the widest varieties of gift cards for purchase. They can be used at various retailers; you can purchase them in physical form or as digital codes. Gift cards offered by Giftcards.com include popular retailers such as Amazon, Target, Best Buy, restaurants, and entertainment venues.

Giftcards.com also offers personalized gift cards and e-gift cards. They allow customers to customize the design and message on the card. In contrast, e-gift cards are digital gift cards delivered via email and can be used online or in-store at participating retailers.

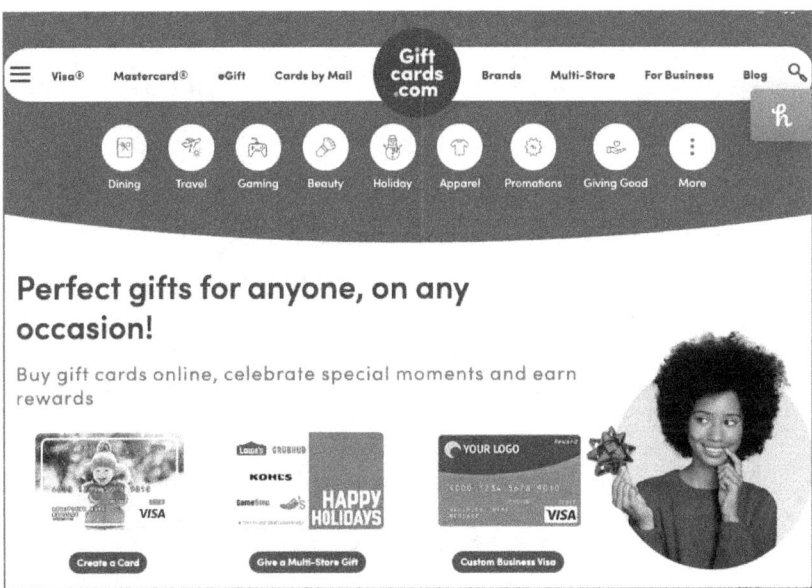

They also offer various gift card exchange services, allowing customers to buy, sell, and trade gift cards. Customers can also check the balance of their gift cards on the website.

NOTE: The App links were not functional at the time of publication.

GIFT CARD PRO #16
Real Deal: Gift Card Granny
Digital Cards: Yes
Mobile App: Yes
Loyalty: Yes
Tracking: Yes

Gift Card Granny has been saving shoppers money since 2009. Known as the "grandmother of all gift cards," their goal is to help you make the best decision when it comes to shopping. Whether buying gift cards or shopping at favorite brands, their team is dedicated to helping save customers money.

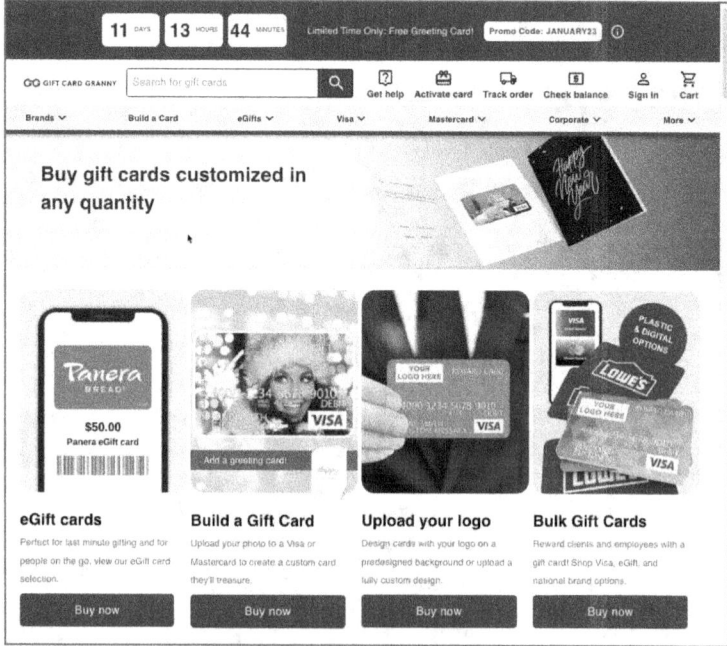

Granny's mission is to (1) make buying gift cards safe, (2) make buying gift cards simple, and (3) help customers save money. All their gift cards have a guaranteed discount or earn you cash back.

GIFT CARD PRO #17

Real Deal: BuyBackWorld

Digital Cards: Yes
Mobile App: No
Loyalty: Yes
Tracking: Yes

With over 400,000 customers, BuyBackWorld allows users to sell their gift cards for cash. The company buys various gift cards from a wide range of retailers and brands and offers competitive prices for the cards it purchases.

To sell a gift card on BuyBackWorld, you'll need to go to the website and search for the retailer or brand of your gift card. Once you've found the appropriate category, enter the card's balance and other relevant information, such as the card's expiration date. BuyBackWorld will then provide you with an offer for your gift card, which you can accept or decline. If you accept the offer, you'll need to provide BuyBackWorld with the card's details and complete the sale.

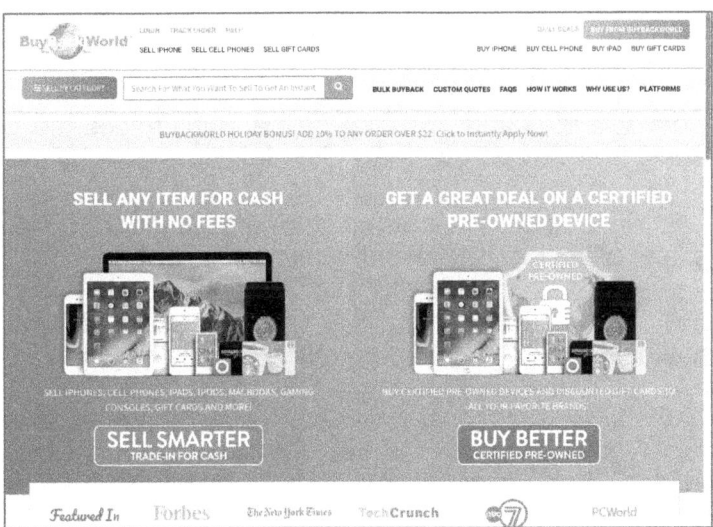

Once the sale is complete, BuyBackWorld will send you payment for your gift card through a check, PayPal payment, or direct deposit, depending on your preference. You can also receive a prepaid shipping label from BuyBackWorld, which you can use to send the gift card to the company.

GIFT CARD PRO #18
Real Deal: GameFlip

Digital Cards: Yes
Mobile App: Yes
Loyalty: Yes
Tracking: Yes

With over 5 million members, GameFlip is a safe marketplace where gamers can find the best deals. Buy and sell games, gift cards, digital items, and movies — or even find a skilled coach to play as your teammate!

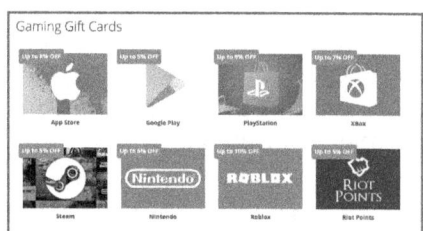

GameFlip is a digital marketplace allowing users to buy and sell various items, including gift cards. Some potential benefits of using GameFlip for gift cards include the following:

1. *Wide variety of options*: GameFlip offers various gift cards from multiple retailers and brands. This means you'll have plenty of options and can find the perfect gift card for any occasion.

2. *Convenient*: GameFlip is an online marketplace, so you can easily browse and purchase gift cards from your home.

3. *Secure*: GameFlip uses safe payment methods to ensure the safety of your personal and financial information.

4. *Easy to use*: GameFlip has a user-friendly interface that makes it easy to find and purchase your desired gift cards.

To use GameFlip to buy or sell gift cards, you must create an account and browse available options. If you're buying a gift card, add it to your cart and check it out using your preferred payment method. You'll need to enter the card's details and set a price if you sell a gift card. Once the sale is complete, you'll receive payment for your gift card through the GameFlip platform.

GIFT CARD PRO #19
Real Deal: Additional Gift Card Platforms

Here are a few other gift card discounters. Browse to find the sites you enjoy and download their mobile app (if available).

Real Deal: SlickDeals.net
Our one-of-a-kind online community and a team of skilled editors are obsessed with uncovering great products and every layer of savings. Users share, confirm, and comment on deals so that everyone benefits.

Real Deal: eBay
Buyers who shop on the ebay.com marketplace, its localized counterparts, and the eBay mobile apps enjoy a highly personalized experience with an unparalleled selection at a value.

Real Deal: Reddit
There are several ways to buy, sell, or trade gift cards on Reddit. Join the subreddit dedicated to buying, selling, or trading gift cards. Several subreddit communities on Reddit focus on buying, selling, or trading gift cards. You can browse these communities to find users interested in purchasing, selling, or trading them. In addition, Reddit offers a free gift card Trading Guide. Download it here.

Real Deal: GiftChill

GiftChill was created as the one-stop shop for online gift card purchases. While other gift card websites exist, they found that they don't accurately cater to the needs of the 21st century. Additionally, tech-savvy users who understand cryptocurrency should be rewarded. By focusing specifically on crypto transactions, they keep overhead low.

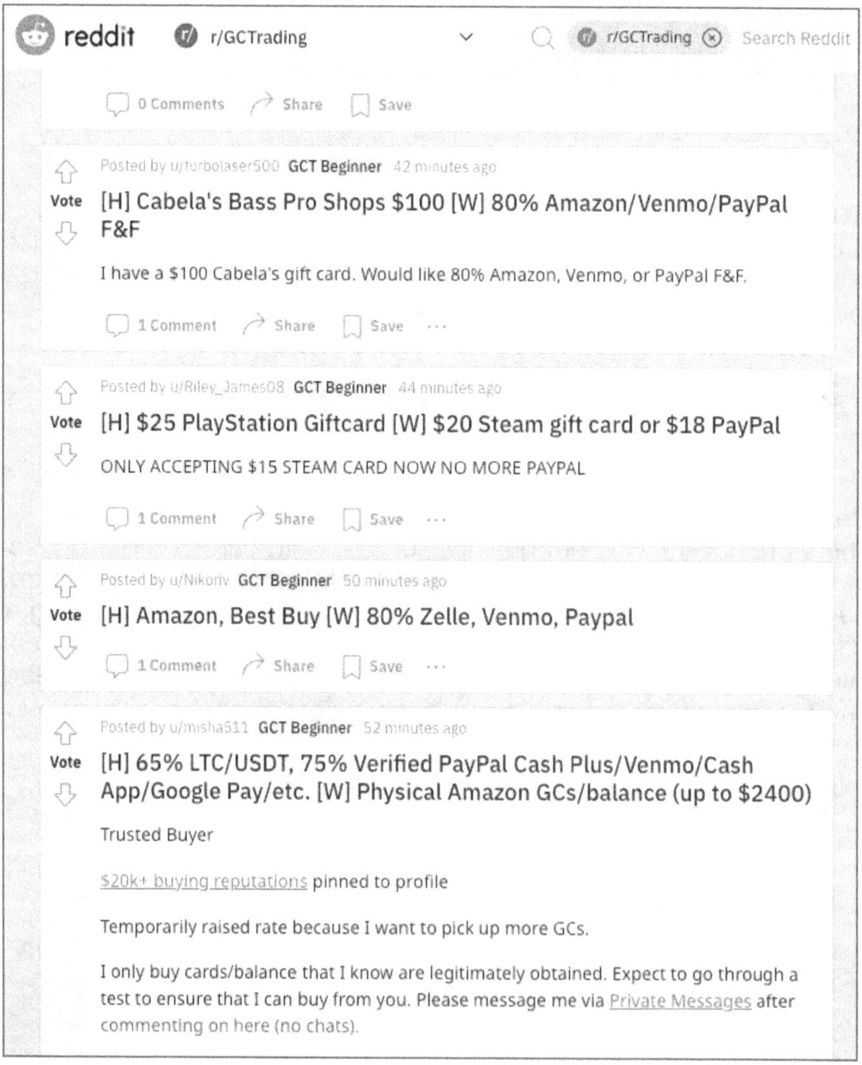

reddit · r/GCTrading ⌄ 🔍 r/GCTrading ✕ Search Reddit

💬 0 Comments ↗ Share 🔖 Save

Posted by u/turbolaser500 **GCT Beginner** 42 minutes ago

Vote **[H] Cabela's Bass Pro Shops $100 [W] 80% Amazon/Venmo/PayPal F&F**

I have a $100 Cabela's gift card. Would like 80% Amazon, Venmo, or PayPal F&F.

💬 1 Comment ↗ Share 🔖 Save ⋯

Posted by u/Riley_James08 **GCT Beginner** 44 minutes ago

Vote **[H] $25 PlayStation Giftcard [W] $20 Steam gift card or $18 PayPal**

ONLY ACCEPTING $15 STEAM CARD NOW NO MORE PAYPAL

💬 1 Comment ↗ Share 🔖 Save ⋯

Posted by u/Nikoriv **GCT Beginner** 50 minutes ago

Vote **[H] Amazon, Best Buy [W] 80% Zelle, Venmo, Paypal**

💬 1 Comment ↗ Share 🔖 Save ⋯

Posted by u/misha511 **GCT Beginner** 52 minutes ago

Vote **[H] 65% LTC/USDT, 75% Verified PayPal Cash Plus/Venmo/Cash App/Google Pay/etc. [W] Physical Amazon GCs/balance (up to $2400)**

Trusted Buyer

$20k+ buying reputations pinned to profile

Temporarily raised rate because I want to pick up more GCs.

I only buy cards/balance that I know are legitimately obtained. Expect to go through a test to ensure that I can buy from you. Please message me via Private Messages after commenting on here (no chats).

Category: Extended Value

This is where you combine other offers for steeper discounts.

GIFT CARD PRO #20
Real Deal: Couponing

Using gift cards and coupons can be an excellent way to save money on purchases. Here are a few tips for maximizing your savings with gift cards and coupons:

1. *Look for discounted gift cards:* You can often find discounted gift cards for popular retailers and restaurants online or in stores. Purchasing a gift card at a discounted price can help you save money on your purchases, even if the gift card has a lower value.

2. *Use coupons and discounts on top of gift cards:* Many retailers and restaurants allow customers to use coupons and discounts for gift card purchases. For example, if you have a $50 gift card for a retailer and a coupon for $10 off your purchase, you can use both the gift card and the coupon to save money on your investment.

3. *Use gift cards and coupons at participating retailers:* Some retailers and restaurants partner with coupon and discount websites, allowing customers to use gift cards and coupons together. For example, if you have a gift card for a retailer and a voucher from a website like RetailMeNot, you can use both the gift card and the coupon at the retailer.

Be sure to check the terms and conditions of the gift card and the coupon to understand any restrictions or limitations on their use.

Top Coupon Apps to Save Money

Coupon apps can help users save money on purchases. Here are a few popular coupon apps:

Coupons.com: This app allows users to find and redeem coupons and discounts from various retailers and restaurants. The app also includes a "nearby" feature.

Honey: This browser extension and the app allow users to find and redeem coupons and discounts from various retailers and restaurants.

Shopkick: This app enables users to earn rewards and discounts from multiple retailers and restaurants by completing tasks such as making purchases, scanning receipts, and visiting stores.

RetailMeNot: This app allows users to find and redeem coupons and discounts from various retailers and restaurants. The app also includes a "nearby" feature that shows users coupons and deals from retailers and restaurants near their current location.

These popular coupon apps can help consumers save money on their purchases. First, however, review the terms and conditions of each app to understand the specific rules and restrictions for earning and redeeming rewards or discounts.

GIFT CARD PRO #21
Real Deal: Loyalty Programs

Initially started by American Airlines in 1981 with their AAdvantage program, loyalty programs are a marketing strategy businesses use to encourage customers to continue shopping at their stores. These programs typically involve retailers offering certain benefits or rewards to customers who shop with them frequently.

Some expected benefits associated with retailer loyalty programs include discounts on purchases, special offers or promotions, early access to sales or new products, and free or discounted shipping. Others may consist of personalized recommendations, exclusive events or experiences, and the ability to earn points or rewards that can be redeemed for merchandise.

Here are a few popular loyalty programs:

1. Starbucks Rewards: Starbucks offers a loyalty program that allows customers to earn "stars" points by making purchases at Starbucks stores. Customers can redeem their stars for rewards, including free food and drinks, merchandise, and Starbucks gift cards.

2. Target Circle: Target's loyalty program allows customers to earn rewards on their purchases at Target stores and Target.com. Rewards can be redeemed for discounts, including future purchases and Target gift cards.

3. Amazon Prime: Amazon's loyalty program offers a variety of benefits to members, including free shipping, access to streaming content, and early access to sales and deals.

4. My Best Buy: Best Buy's loyalty program allows customers to earn points on their purchases at Best Buy stores and BestBuy.com. Points can be redeemed for various rewards, including discounts on upcoming purchases and Best Buy gift cards.

5. <u>Macy's Star Rewards</u>: Macy's loyalty program allows customers to earn points on their purchases at Macy's stores and Macys.com. Points can be redeemed for various rewards, including discounts on future purchases and Macy's gift cards.

6. <u>Walgreens Balance Rewards</u>: Walgreens' loyalty program allows customers to earn points on their purchases at Walgreens stores and Walgreens.com.

7. <u>Kohl's Yes2You Rewards</u>: Kohl's loyalty program enables customers to earn points on their purchases at Kohl's stores and Kohls.com.

8. <u>Bed Bath & Beyond+</u>: Bed Bath & Beyond's loyalty program offers a variety of benefits to members, including 20% off all purchases and free shipping. Members can also purchase Bed Bath & Beyond gift cards on the website.

9. <u>Home Depot Pro Xtra</u>: Home Depot's loyalty program for professionals offers a variety of benefits, including discounts on purchases, access to exclusive deals, and the ability to earn and redeem points for Home Depot gift cards.

10. <u>Lowe's Business Rewards</u>: Lowe's loyalty program for businesses provides various benefits, including discounts on purchases, access to exclusive deals, and the ability to earn and redeem points for Lowe's gift cards.

Conduct a simple Google search to find your favorite retailers to see if they offer a Loyalty Program.

GIFT CARD PRO #22
Real Deal: Receipts to Gift Cards

The following app is quite popular because your receipts can get extended value. Convert receipts to gift cards, depending on the retailer or business where the receipt was issued.

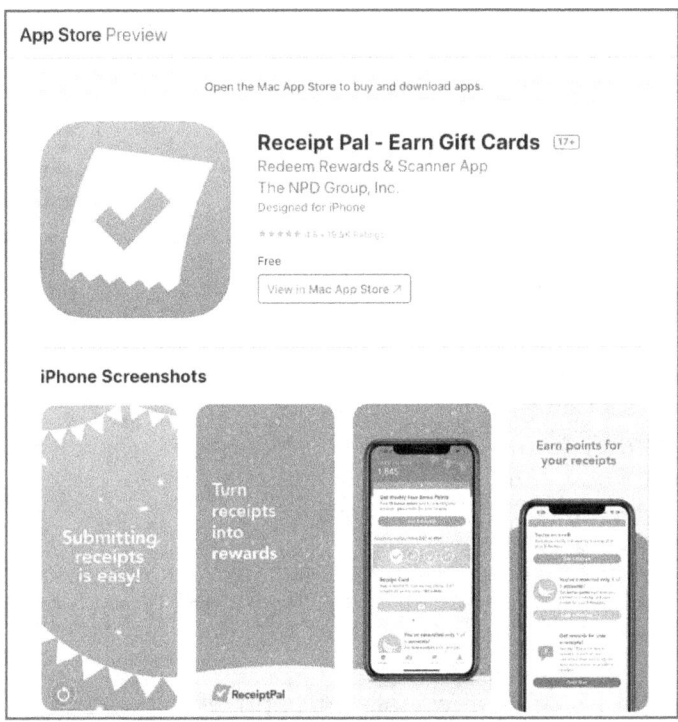

Receipt Pal app
ReceiptPal: This app is for you if you want to earn gift cards and prizes from retailers like Amazon, Chili's, Walmart, Target, Home Depot, and Applebees. Take a pic and submit your paper receipts for credit. You can earn 100 points for each complete green Point Card. Redeem your points for gift cards at retailers in your area.

GIFT CARD PRO #23

Real Deal: Survey Says!

Several websites and apps offer gift cards as a reward for taking surveys or completing other tasks, such as visiting sites, watching videos, or participating in focus groups. Some popular platforms that offer gift cards as a reward include:

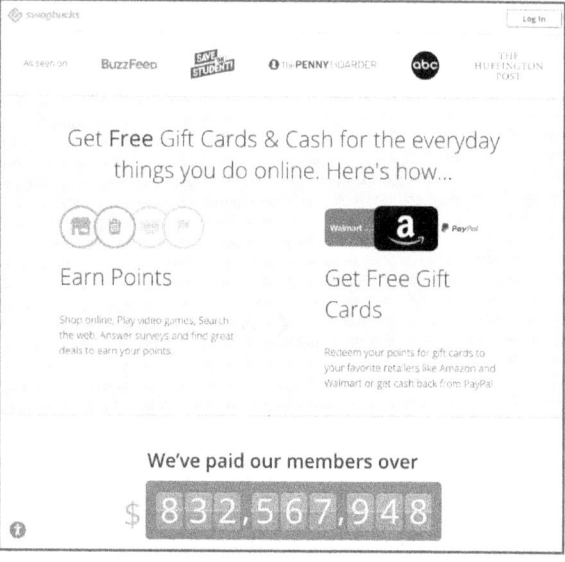

- Survey Junkie: Users earn points by completing surveys and participating in focus groups. The points can be redeemed for gift cards for popular retailers like Amazon, Best Buy, and Target and cash via PayPal.

- Ipsos i-Say: Their website and app allow users to earn points by completing surveys and participating in polls. The points can be redeemed for gift cards for popular retailers such as Walmart, Starbucks, Home Depot, and Petco and cash via PayPal.

- MyPoints: Earn points by completing surveys, shopping online, and more.

- American Consumer Opinion: This website allows users to earn points by completing surveys and participating in focus groups.

- Swagbucks: They allow users to earn points by completing surveys, watching videos, shopping online, and more.

- Pinecone Research: Users earn points by completing surveys and participating in product testing.

Many websites and apps offer points that can be converted to gift cards as a reward for taking surveys and participating in other tasks. These platforms can be a good option for individuals earning gift cards or cash by participating in market research studies.

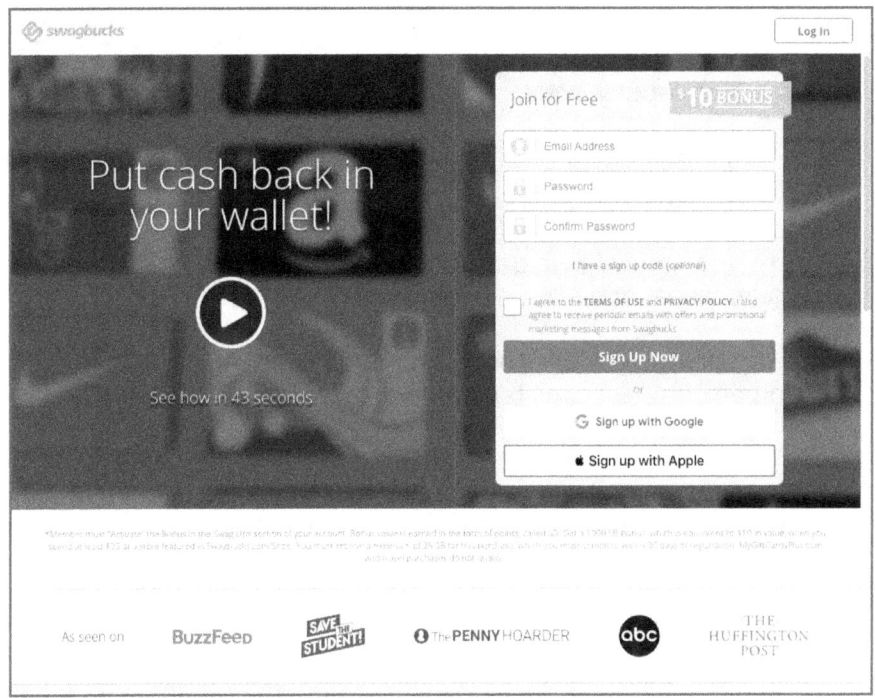

GIFT CARD PRO #24
Real Deal: Cash-Back Credit Cards

Purchasing discounted gift cards with cash-back credit cards allows users to leverage their savings, including buying gift cards.

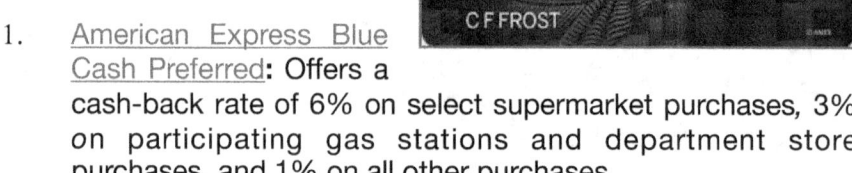

Here are a few popular ones:

1. American Express Blue Cash Preferred: Offers a cash-back rate of 6% on select supermarket purchases, 3% on participating gas stations and department store purchases, and 1% on all other purchases.

2. Capital One Quicksilver: Offers a flat cash-back rate of 1.5% on all purchases, with no annual fee.

3. Citi Double Cash: Provides a cash-back rate of 1% on all purchases and an additional 1% when users pay off their balance. There is no annual fee for this card.

4. Chase Freedom Unlimited: Offers a flat cash-back rate of 1.5% on all purchases, with no annual fee.

5. Discover it Cash Back: Provides rotating categories in which users can earn 5% cash back on their purchases and a flat 1% cash-back rate on all other purchases. In addition, there is no annual fee for this card.

These are a few popular credit cards that allow users to earn cash back on their purchases. Be sure to compare the features and fees of each one to find the one that is the best fit for your needs and spending habits.

Category: Locals Only

GIFT CARD PRO #25
Real Deal: Meeting-in-Person

Trading gift cards online with established merchants is relatively easy and safe, but trading gift cards locally is somewhat different. Online marketplaces such as Craigslist or FB Marketplace can result in in-person meetings.

Protecting yourself and ensuring the transaction goes smoothly is essential when this occurs. According to Craigslist, here are a few precautions you should take when buying or selling anything in person:

1. *Use a secure payment method.* If this is a cash deal, this wouldn't be applicable.

2. *Meet in a public place.* When arranging to meet with someone to buy or sell a gift card, it's a good idea to meet in a public area. This can reduce the risk of fraud or other problems and provide a safer environment for the transaction.

3. *Use caution with personal information.* Be careful about sharing personal information, such as your address or phone number, with someone you buy or sell from on Craigslist.

4. *Trust your instincts.* If you have doubts or concerns about a transaction, trust your instincts and consider canceling the deal. Better to be safe than sorry.

Following these precautions can reduce the risk of fraud or other problems and have a smoother, more successful transaction. If you met the gift card reseller via Facebook Marketplace, consider leaving a review.

GIFT CARD PRO #26
Real Deal: Craigslist

Craigslist is a platform that allows users to buy, sell, and exchange gift cards. Here are a few reasons why someone might want to buy, sell, or trade gift cards there:

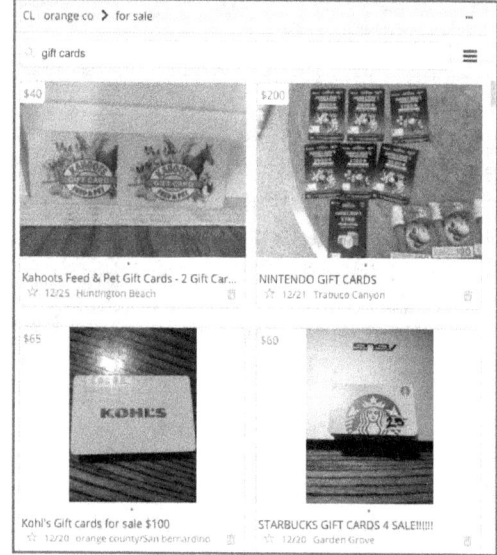

1. *Local transactions:* Craigslist is a regional platform, meaning buyers and sellers are typically located in the same geographic area. This can make it easier to arrange in-person transactions and avoid shipping fees.

2. *Large selection:* Craigslist has a large user base, which can make it easier to find a wide variety of gift card offers.

3. *Negotiability:* Because Craigslist is a platform for individual buyers and sellers, it can be easier to negotiate the terms of a gift card transaction. This can be especially useful when buying a gift card at a discount or selling a gift card for a higher price.

Here are a few examples of gift card offers and savings you might find on Craigslist:

1. A $50 Amazon gift card for $40

2. A $100 Target gift card for $80

3. A $25 Starbucks gift card in exchange for a $25 Target card

GIFT CARD PRO #27
Real Deal: Facebook Marketplace

Facebook Marketplace is a popular platform year-round for trading gift cards.

The marketplace offers a large user base, convenience, and community feedback. I have noticed that some sellers will only describe the card's value, not the card's restrictions. It's always wise to ask for details before committing to a purchase. For example, some gift cards have conditions such as online or in-store purchases only.

A clear advantage of using Facebook is its highly targeted ad platform. This could also benefit those who wish to trade for a profit.

Remember to be careful when buying, selling, or trading gift cards on Facebook Marketplace or any other platform. Follow all relevant guidelines and rules, and use a secure payment method to protect yourself. Research any seller or trade partner before making a transaction to ensure they are reputable and trustworthy.

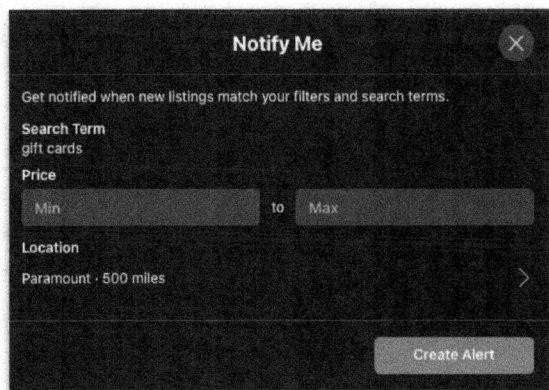

GIFT CARD PRO #28
Real Deal: Big Box Trade-Ins

You can trade your old electronics for gift cards at participating Target and Best Buy stores and other retail locations. Some retailers such as Target, Walmart, and Best Buy have similar trade-in programs because they use Assurant as their official vendor to operate the program.

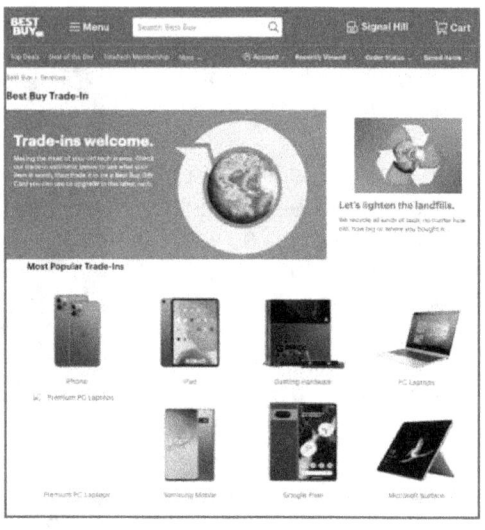

Customers provide information about the items they want to trade in, such as the make and model, and the exchange will provide a quote for the trade-in value. Then, if the customer agrees to the selection, they send the items for inspection. If the condition is as described, the exchange will issue a digital gift card for the trade-in value.

Note: The items accepted for trade-in differ among retailers, so it's best to check around.

Target Tech Trade-In
Target trade-in accepts mobile phones, tablets, wearables, MP3 players, video games and consoles, and smart speakers. This includes Apple devices such as iPhones, iPads, and Apple Watches. Begin the process online or at the electronics department inside the store.

Best Buy Trade-in
Best Buy's program allows customers to trade in eligible items, such as electronics, video games, and movies, for a Best Buy gift card. You must be 18 or older (except in AL or NE, 19 or older) to take advantage of the program. The Trade-In Program is unavailable at all locations; check their website for the nearest participating store.

GameStop

The retailer accepts game consoles, video games, controllers, smartphones, tablets, wearables, and even headphones. You can select between cash and GameStop credit if the product is accepted.

Walmart Trade-In

Accepts a wide variety of electronics and other products, and it's a quick process. (1) Find your device and answer a few questions. (2) Ship it to CExchange with a pre-paid shipping label you print from your printer. Shipping is via FedEx Ground and is free. (3) You're sent a Walmart eGift card upon product evaluation.

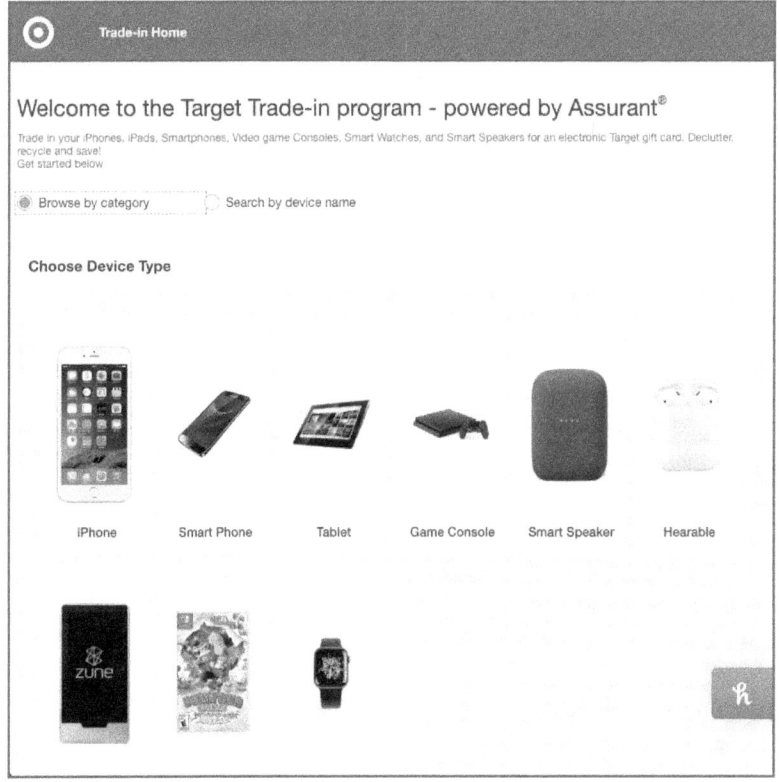

GIFT CARD PRO #29
Real Deal: Cash-out Redemption

In certain states, you can liquidate the remaining gift card balance for actual cash. Sadly, not every state offers this benefit.

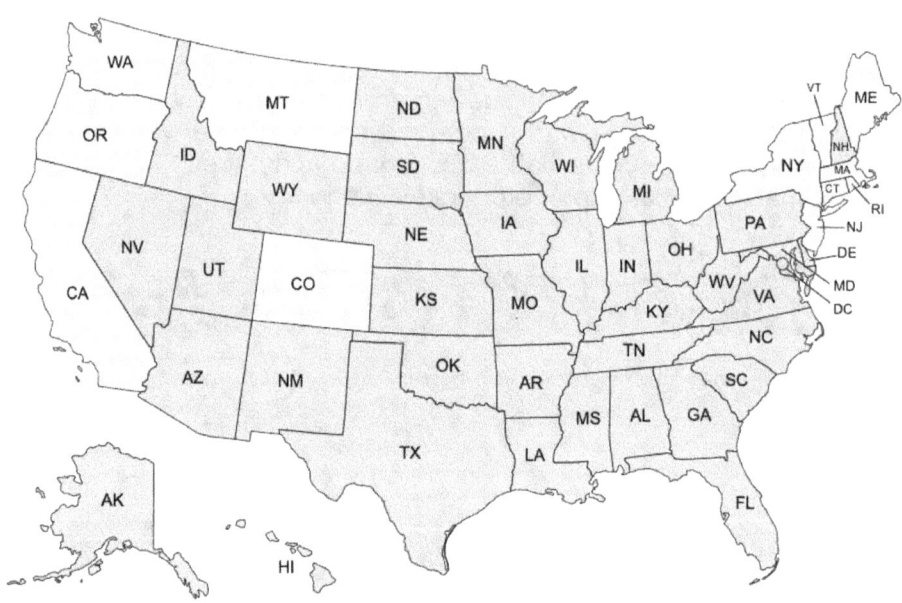

California: $10 or less
Colorado: Less than $5
Connecticut: Less than $3
Maine: Less than $5
Massachusetts: Less than 90% of original card value
Montana: Less than $5
New Jersey: Less than $5
New York: Less than $5
Oregon: Less than $5
Rhode Island: Less than $1
Washington: Less than $5
Vermont: Less than $1

Gift Card Pro #30
Real Deal: Amazon for Cash

There are a few ways you can sell an Amazon gift card for cash:

1. **Sell the gift card to a gift card exchange service:** Popular gift card exchange services include CardCash and Raise. Several online exchange services allow you to sell your Amazon gift card for cash. These services typically offer a lower price than its face value, but they are a convenient and quick way to sell your gift card.

2. **Sell the gift card on a peer-to-peer marketplace:** You can also sell your Amazon gift card on a peer-to-peer marketplace such as eBay or Reddit. Create an account on the platform and list your gift card, setting the price and terms of the sale. Then, wait for a buyer to purchase your gift card and complete the transaction.

3. **Sell the gift card to a friend or family member:** If you have someone in your life who would be interested in your Amazon gift card, you can try selling it to them for cash. You can negotiate the price and terms of the sale with the person directly.

4. **Sell the gift card to a local store that buys gift cards:** Some local stores and pawn shops will purchase gift cards for money, although at a lower price than the face value of the card. Use Google Maps for stores in your area.

5. **Use the gift card to purchase items you can resell:** You can also use your Amazon gift card to buy items you can then resell for cash. This option requires more effort and time, as you must find buyers for the items you purchase.

These are a few additional ideas for selling an Amazon gift card for cash. It is essential to carefully consider the terms and fees of any service or platform you use to sell your gift card and the risks and benefits of each option.

GIFT CARD PRO #31
Real Deal: Amazon Trade-Ins

According to the Amazon website: "The Trade-In program allows customers to receive an Amazon.com Gift Card in exchange for thousands of eligible items including Amazon Devices, cell phones, video games, and more. Some trade-ins may also be eligible for a limited-time, promotional credit off a new qualifying Amazon Devices."

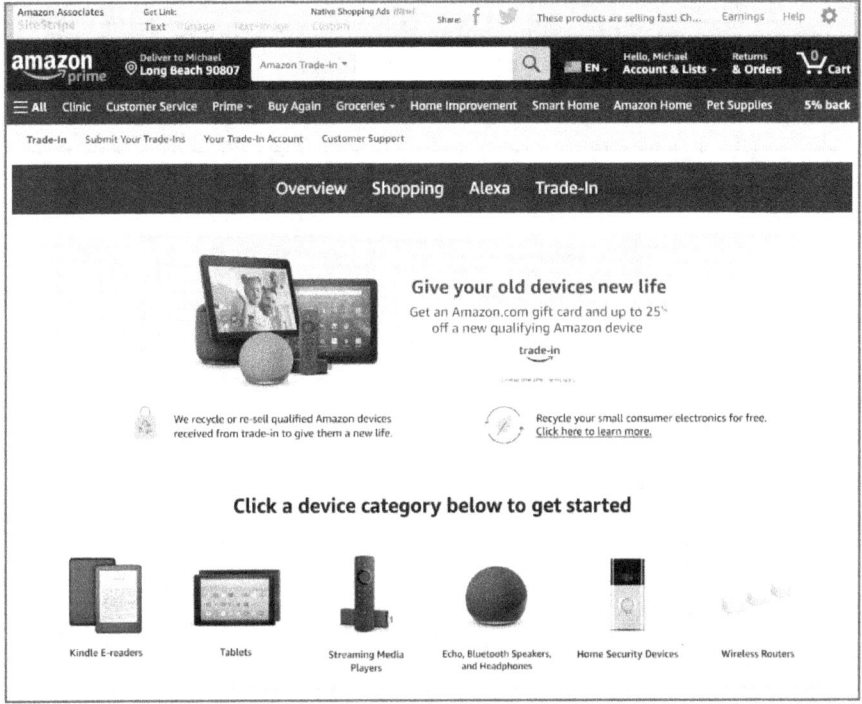

Curious about what is accepted as a trade-in? Eligible items for trade-in are listed on the Trade-In Store and can be searched within the 'Find more items' button and within the 'Upgrade and save with Trade-In' button on select new device pages. If your item is not listed in one of these locations, then they currently do not have an offer for it. The Trade-In program is constantly updated with new items, so check back regularly.

GIFT CARD PRO #32
Real Deal: V-MC to Amazon

If you have a general-purpose card such as a Visa, MasterCard, or American Express with a low balance, you can convert the amount to an Amazon gift card for the remaining balance on the card. For example, let's say you have a Visa gift card for $5.06. Then, log into Amazon and add the total value remaining balance.

Best Seller

Amazon.com eGift Card
$1⁰⁰ - $2,000⁰⁰   Amazon brand

Amazon.com Gift Card in a Mini Envelope
$10⁰⁰ - $2,000⁰⁰   Amazon brand

Amazon's Choice

Amazon.com Gift Card in a Holiday Gift Box (Various Designs)
$25⁰⁰ - $2,000⁰⁰   Amazon brand

GIFT CARD PRO #33
Real Deal: Purse.io

If you possess Bitcoin or Bitcoin Cash and want to save money shopping on Amazon, you can exchange the crypto for discounted items when you shop on the platform; your order is matched with an earner.

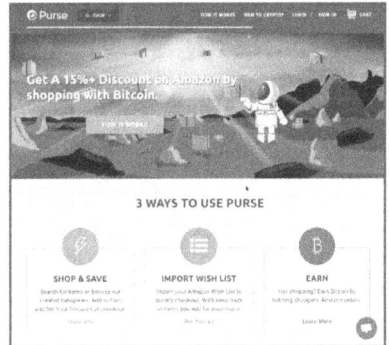

Earners own Amazon gift cards and will fulfill your order in return for your cryptocurrency.

Shoppers enjoy a discount for providing this opportunity, while Purse ensures this process is smooth and frictionless.

By paying with cryptocurrency, shoppers receive a deal and earners cash in their gift cards. Here's an in-depth video on how to utilize purse.io.

Purse has three ways:

1. SHOP & SAVE: Search for items or browse the curated categories. Then, add to the cart and set your discount at checkout.

2. IMPORT WISH LIST: Quickly import an Amazon Wish List to the checkout. Purse will keep track of items added for easy reuse.

3. EARN: Not shopping? Earn Bitcoin by fulfilling shoppers' Amazon orders.

Without cryptocurrency, Purse cannot match you with an earner looking to purchase orders in exchange for coins. Send funds to your Purse wallet and start shopping.

You can select a discount amount. Ensure your slider is set to 5% on the left for the fastest delivery. For more savings, move the slider right until you are satisfied. You can also modify your discount after placing your order, so long as an earner has not picked it up. Earners will exchange their Amazon gift cards for your cryptocurrency by seeking a good order and funding it through Purse.

Category: Miscellaneous

GIFT CARD PRO #34
Real Deal: Terms & Conditions

All gift cards are bound by what is referred to as Terms & Conditions, which basically explain how the card can be used. Here are some examples of terms and conditions that may be included on gift cards:

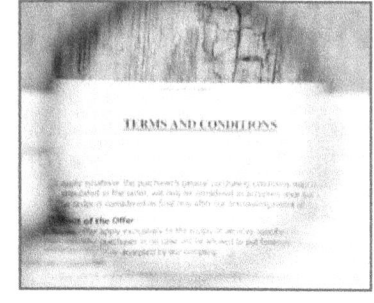

1. *Expiration date*: Some gift cards may have an expiration date, after which the card will no longer be valid, and the remaining balance will be forfeited.

2. *Fees*: Selected gift cards may have expenses, such as activation fees, service fees, or inactivity fees. These fees may be charged on a monthly or annual basis and can reduce the value of the gift card over time.

3. *Restrictions*: Gift cards may have restrictions, such as where they can be used, what they can be used to purchase, or <u>the amount of gift card value per transaction</u>.

4. *Redeem-ability*: Cards may only be redeemable in specific locations or certain channels, such as online or in-store.

5. *Replacement*: Some gift cards may have policies for replacing lost or stolen cards, although these can vary significantly.

6. *Customization:* There are additional fees associated with customization, such as adding a personal message or image to the card.

7. *Returns and exchanges*: Gift cards may have policies in place for returns and exchanges.

It's important to carefully read the terms and conditions of a gift card before purchasing or using it, as these terms and conditions can affect the value and usability of the card.

GIFT CARD PRO #35
Real Deal: Gift Card Cross Exchange

If you have a gift card that you don't want or need, you might be able to exchange it for another gift card that is more useful to you. Here are some steps you can take to exchange a gift card for another one:

1. Check the gift card's terms and conditions: Before you try to exchange a gift card, understand its terms and conditions. Some gift cards may have restrictions on when or where they can be used, or they may have expiration dates.

2. Find a gift card exchange website or app: Several websites and apps allow you to exchange gift cards. Some popular options include CardCash, Raise, and Gift Card Granny. Read reviews and check the reputation of the website or app you choose.

3. Enter your gift card information: Once you've selected a gift card exchange website or app, enter the card details you want to exchange. This typically includes the card number, expiration date, and security code.

4. Choose the gift card you wish to receive: After you've entered your information, you can choose the gift card you want to receive in exchange. Make sure to select a gift card that you know you'll use and that has a similar value to the one you're exchanging.

5. Complete the exchange: Once you've chosen the gift card you want to receive, you'll need to complete the sale by following the instructions provided by the website or app. This may involve sending your gift card to the exchange company or providing proof of ownership.

6. Use your new gift card: After the exchange, you should receive your new one. Make sure to use it before any expiration dates, and enjoy your new purchase!

It's important to note that some gift cards may not be eligible for exchange, or you may only be able to exchange them for a percentage of their original value. So make sure to read the terms and conditions carefully and do your research before attempting to exchange a gift card.

GIFT CARD PRO #36

Real Deal: Donate to Charity

Donating gift cards to charity can be a great way to give back and support a cause you care about. **Help those in need and support a cause you care about.** If you have a particular reason or issue you are passionate about, donating gift cards to a charity supporting that cause can be a meaningful way to make a difference.

GIFT CARD PRO #37

Real Deal: Regifting

Regifting a gift card is the practice of giving a gift card you received as a gift to someone else. While regifting can be a convenient and cost-effective way to give a gift, there are a few things to consider before going ahead:

- *Ensure the gift card is appropriate for the recipient.* Consider the recipient's interests, preferences, and needs before regifting a gift card. The giver didn't consider it. That's why you're probably regifting the gift card in the first place.

- *Check the expiration date.* Some gift cards have expiration dates, so it is essential to check the terms and conditions before regifting the gift card to ensure that it will only expire after it can be used.

- *Consider the gift card's value.* If the gift card is low, keeping it for personal use or using it as a stocking stuffer might be more appropriate than regifting it.

Regifting a gift card can be an easy and inexpensive means to give a gift. Still, it is essential to consider the recipient's interests and needs, the expiration date, and the gift card's value.

GIFT CARD PRO #38
Real Deal: Loose Change for Gift Cards

Founded in 1991, Coinstar has operated kiosks in grocery stores and other retail locations, allowing customers to exchange their loose change for cash. Coinstar kiosks accept a wide variety of coins, including pennies, nickels, dimes, and quarters, and users can choose to receive their money in the form of a cash voucher or a gift card.

GIFT CARD PRO #39
Real Deal: Gift Card Scams

Over $534 billion in gift cards were sold last year. That averages to about $14.6 billion on gift cards every single day. Most people think they are sold mainly during the holiday season, but they are popular all year round. Gift cards a given for birthdays, anniversaries, graduations, and other celebrations throughout the year.

Unfortunately, with this much money on the line, scammers do everything possible to trick and defraud consumers. Below is a list of common gift card scams and how to avoid getting ripped off.

1. *Phishing scams:* Scammers send fake emails or text messages that appear to be from a legitimate company, asking for personal information to redeem a gift card or offer a gift card as a reward for providing personal information. To avoid this common gift card scam, do not click on links or enter personal information in response to unsolicited messages.

2. *Card swapping*: Fraudsters tamper with gift card racks at retail stores such as CVS or Rite Aid, swapping out legitimate cards for ones with lower or no value. The most common is adding a label with a barcode over the gift card's existing barcode—so you're activating another card, not the one being purchased. Inspect gift cards before buying them to

circumvent these schemes and ensure they have not been tampered with. Lastly, check the receipt for any inaccuracies,

3. *Unsolicited phone calls*: Scammers call and claim to be from a legitimate company, offering a gift card or asking for payment information to redeem one. To dodge these rip-offs, only provide personal information or make payments over the phone if you initiated the call and know the company's legitimacy.

4. *Online marketplace fraud:* Sadly, scammers sell counterfeit or non-existent gift cards online. To circumvent these schemes, only purchase gift cards from trusted retailers and be suspicious of deals that seem too good to be true.

5. *Card pooling:* Look out for scammers who ask individuals to contribute money towards bulk purchasing gift cards but then take the money and wait to deliver the cards. To dodge these rip-offs, do not participate in card pooling schemes; only purchase gift cards directly from trusted retailers or legitimate online gift card resellers.

6. *Social media scams*: Scammers create fake social media accounts or posts, offering gift cards in exchange for personal information or money. To avoid these scams, only provide personal information or send money to social media accounts if you know they are legitimate.

7. *In-person scams*: Scammers approach people in public places, offering gift cards or asking for payment in exchange for a gift card. To elude these cons, only provide personal information or make payments to individuals you know.

8. *Unscrupulous gift card resellers*: Scammers may purchase gift cards from legitimate retailers and resell them at a discounted price on online marketplaces. To fend off these frauds, be cautious about buying gift cards from resellers and ensure the card has yet to be previously redeemed.

9. *Card-not-present fraud*: Scammers steal gift card numbers and use them to make fraudulent purchases online. Keep secure gift card numbers and PINs to ward off these deceptions, and check the card's balance regularly.

10. *Card-testing*: Online scammers use automated tools to test large numbers of gift card numbers and balances to identify the ones that are still active and have a balance. To avoid these scams, monitor your gift card balance regularly and report any suspicious activity or unauthorized transactions to the gift card issuer.

Conclusion

Well, I would like to thank you for reading this publication. Your support of *Gift Card Pro* is genuinely appreciated.

If you've read this far, you are now in the top 1% who know about gift cards and how to benefit from them. The next step is to conduct your research to determine the resources that meet your needs. There's plenty to choose from, whether discount traders, extended value, Amazon, or other gift card strategies. So take action to start profiting from the gift card economy today.

Congratulations, you have now become a *Gift Card Pro*!

Gift Card Pro Links

Use your mobile device to scan the QR code; you can download a PDF file containing all the links within the paperback book.

Gift Card Pro Updates

As you well know, the gift card industry has evolved quickly and is making changes accordingly. To ensure you're up-to-date, please visit: https://www.ImportantAdvice.com/updates